THE
BIRDER'S
JOURNAL

Bob Waldon
editorial consultant

Waterlane
editions

Vancouver/Toronto

THE
BIRDER'S
JOURNAL

Bob Waldon
editorial consultant

Waterlane
e d i t i o n s

Vancouver/Toronto

The information in this book is true and complete to the best of our
knowledge. All recommendations are made without guarantee on the part
of the author or Waterlane Editions. The author and publisher disclaim
any liability in connection with the use of this information. For additional
information, please contact Waterlane Editions, 351 Lynn Avenue, North
Vancouver, B.C. V7J 2C4.

Cover and interior design: Antonia Banyard

Printed and bound in Canada by Friesens, Altona, Manitoba.

Canadian Cataloguing in Publication Data
Waldon, Bob, 1932—
The birder's journal

ISBN 1-55110-773-2

1. Bird watching. I. Title.
QL676.W34 1998   598.07'234   C98-910662-4

*The publisher acknowledges the support of the Canada Council for the Arts and the Cultural
Services Branch of the Government of British Columbia for our publishing program. We
acknowledge the financial support of the Government of Canada through the Book Industry
Development Program for our publishing activities.*

Contents

THE BASICS
OF BIRDING

What?

Birds have an almost universal appeal. Their beauty and song add pleasure to even fleeting encounters. It is when people go beyond casual contact, and actively seek out birds, or feed and house them, that they begin the transformation into "birders." They will not be long into this process before discovering that there are many others who share their interest. The international fascination with birds has turned them into the basis of a major recreational phenomenon. Bird feeding is second only to gardening as the most popular outdoor pastime, and birding is the backbone of the thriving eco-tourism industry.

Welcome to the world of birds and birding!

Where?

Habitat is where it's at; everything else is secondary. If you insist on looking for ducks in the desert and roadrunners in the marsh, good luck! Remember that the edges of habitats, where two different eco-zones meet, appeal to birds—river banks, lake shores, the sun-warming sides of groves at dawn, the edges where meadows meet shrubbery. Don't hurry, move softly, pause often, and use binoculars.

The aware birder quickly becomes "hot spot" attuned. Hot spots are places of special attraction for certain species of birds and all species of birders. You don't have to fly to Colombia or the Galapagos Islands for action. Some of the best hot spots are in or near big cities. Sewage lagoons, reservoirs, beaches before and after summer, parks, and minimum-spray golf courses can be great. Don't ignore your own yard, especially if you feed birds and/or live near some natural habitat.

When?

Early on a spring morning. By getting out at dawn, you will catch
birds busy with breakfast, singing their heads off. You can go birding all year, but spring migration is the most exciting time. The
males are in bright mating plumage and the leaves aren't yet out to
block the view. In contrast, autumn birds are in non-breeding drab
colors and most don't sing. Sorting out fall migrants is a challenge
with awesome potential for frustration.

How?

Do it. If you're new, join a club, sign on for outings, seek advice.
Bird walk leaders respond well to questions. Keep notes. Then try it
on your own, often. Use your ears. Get a tape or CD of bird songs
and calls. Learn to know birds by sound as well as sight.

Why?

You get a front-row seat at nature's real-life drama, and you entertain
yourself while acquiring knowledge. You will also gain friendships,
little shared triumphs, or nature photography skills. Maybe, in time,
you'll even add a little to our overall store of scientific knowledge.
What better reasons are there?

*Rubbing at dust or finger marks on camera
and binocular lenses with tissue paper will
scratch the coating. Buy a lens cleaning kit
from a camera store or an optician.*

The Birder's Tools

Binoculars

Someone wearing comfortable clothing and absorbed in searching for something in the trees is likely a birder. But the clinching field mark is the binoculars. Binoculars add a touch of magic as they suddenly bring a little brown bird into arms-length close-up, vivid with unexpected color and patterns.

How much does the magic cost? For throwing into the glove compartment, fifty dollars. For a set you'll hang around your neck and peer through all day, better go for a hundred and up. State-of-the-art? Would you believe thousands? Between the extremes there are infinite choices. Start your quest with a magazine from a nature or a book store. Scan the ads and set your low-high price limits. Then shop.

Basic Rules: Try them and don't rush. Look for clear images, sharp lines from close-up to infinity. Do they feel right, with smooth but firm controls that you can use with thick gloves? Get long (15 mm or ⅝ inch) eye relief if you'll use them with glasses. The closer they focus, the better they'll be for feeder watching. Don't assume that units of the same model off the same assembly line are identical. They're not, so try the ones you buy.

Size: Compacts—Light weight, shirt pocket friendly, but a narrower field of vision, lower image brightness in dim light than standards. Standards—wider field and a brighter image in poor light, weight could be painful after a few hours of use, but a light shoulder harness designed to carry cameras and binoculars can relieve "birder's neck."

Power: The description "7 x 35" means a bird will appear about seven times closer and "35" is the diameter of the object lens in millimeters. The bigger the lens, the brighter the image—an advantage in dim light, but not a good feature in bright sun or snow. Don't go power-happy—you'll get a clearer image with a good 7-power than with a shabby 10. Cheap zoom? Forget it. Good zoom? Pay more.

Field Guide

A good guide is an essential birding tool. All the major guides are good. It saves a lot of page flipping if the range maps are on the same page as the illustrations and descriptions.

Notebook

A hardcover notebook is durable and provides its own writing surface. This book should fit into a shirt or jacket pocket. Spiral bound books are another option. Choose a pencil that is slim enough to be carried in the spine or coil.

Day Pack

Your pack should include extra clothing for rain or cold, space to stash clothing when it gets hot, aspirin, toilet paper, sunscreen, lunch (& the scraps!), juice, Band-Aids, film, sunglasses, insect repellent, lens cleaner, etc.

Clothing

Get a jacket with a hood that is waterproof, not "showerproof" or "water resistant," and big enough to fit over a bulky sweater if necessary. A roomy vest loaded with pockets is also great. A baseball cap lets ears and neck burn, and the stiff peak gets in the way when you use your binoculars. Find a hat with an all-round, soft brim.

Birding Abroad

The opportunities for participating in outings, tours, and trips have become virtually limitless in the last few years. But while a trip to far-off places is exciting, don't be in a hurry to rush off. Give yourself time to get to know your local birds first. Then, when you do start traveling, this basic knowledge will greatly enhance your pleasure in the new birds you'll see. If you've already joined a local naturalist and/or bird club, fellow members will have their own favorite spots to tell you about. Their newsletters will also advertize trips and destinations for birders.

You can contact the National Audubon Society in the U.S., the American Birding Association, or the Canadian Nature Federation in Canada for lists of their affiliated clubs. You might also call the nearest bird feeding specialty store, which can be either an independent or a member of a chain such as Wild Birds Unlimited, Wild Birds Nature Shop, Wild Bird Centers, and others. Many of these shops not only sell a wealth of birding gear and information sources, they may host lectures and workshops and offer trips.

North American Destinations

Point Pelee (Ontario), Florida, the Texas Gulf Coast, Cape May (New Jersey), Hawk Mountain (Pennsylvania), and many other places are legendary destinations for birders in North America.

Wherever you choose to go, keep in mind that most tours involve getting up early. You will spend less time driving and more time birding (or sleeping) if you stay overnight close to the site. Reserving well in advance is a good idea if your destination is any distance from a major city.

Then there are bird festivals. You can take in the Kachemak Bay Shorebird Festival in Homer, Alaska, the Osprey Festival in Creston, British Columbia, the Loon Festival in Walker Lake, Nevada, or the Festival of the Cranes in Socorro, New Mexico, and so on. There are around 150 to choose from.

The proliferation of these celebrations is driven by a variety of motives, the most prevalent being to boost local tourism. Certainly all of them strive to give visitors a good time, but their value as birding events bears investigation. A suggested first step is to get a copy of the Directory of Birding Festivals, which is updated every year. Contact the festivals that look the most interesting, and ask them how much actual birding there is and what the area offers in the way of good birding sites.

World Destinations

Eco-tourism is now big business. You can book a cruise to the Antarctic to look at the penguins, or take a plane or wilderness train ride to Churchill, Manitoba to view the birds or polar bears that loaf away the summer there. Costa Rica, Belize, the Galapagos Islands, and other exotic parts of the globe are major birding destinations.

Package tours might not appeal to everyone's sense of daring and adventure, but they are a good way of getting to know that

---

The Americas are home to the world's smallest flying bird, the Bee Hummingbird of Cuba, which weighs, on average, 1.6 grams (0.056 oz.) —285 of these birds would weigh a pound.

dream destination. The alternative—traveling, sheltering, feeding, and possibly medicating yourself in a foreign language and with unfamiliar money—may give you some great stories. But for many of us it is altogether the wrong kind of excitement.

Good tour operators will give you the lowdown on visas, immunization shots, currency, health/accident insurance, customs regulations, what to wear, what not to eat, etc. They will, in effect, take care of most of the hassles, leaving you free to enjoy the pleasures.

Which tour operator? The established ones get repeat business by offering good service. That service, however, reflects widely differing client demands. Some hardy travelers aren't concerned about creature comforts as long as they get those prized birds. Unless you are prepared to find out what "modest accommodation" really means in an unfamiliar country, seek the counsel of friends with experience.

The tour operator you finally sign up with can also suggest, and perhaps sell, travel manuals, history books, and bird field guides to the country of your destination. The armchair travel and birding you do in advance will heighten pre-departure anticipation and, once you're there, enable you to get much more out of your all-too-brief sojourn.

About 645 species of birds live or breed in North America north of the Mexican border. Another 50 or so are occasional migrants or regular visitors.

Feeding Birds

Why Feed?

There are two sets of benefits to feeding birds, one for the birds, one for you. Your feed will help more birds survive the winter and resist disease and parasites. In severe weather you may save some from outright starvation.

Aside from a glow of benevolence, you will also give yourself a front-row seat in the drama of everyday survival, a special miracle where winters are severe. And when birding is an everyday event, you become a sharper observer when you are out in the field, better at sorting out field marks or learning calls and songs. You will also find yourself wondering how birds' highly specialized bodies and behavior enable them to cope with environmental challenges.

Feeding birds means they seek you out. This role reversal lets you watch and study them in comfort, with your camera, binoculars, field guide, and coffee all within reach.

Why Not Feed?

An honest appraisal of feeding birds should acknowledge its negative side. It can be a bother to put up feeders, fill them and clean them. There's often messy spilled seeds, husks, and droppings. Party crashers like starlings and pigeons and unwelcome visitors like rats, mice, squirrels, and raccoons may be drawn to the tasty seed. Others, possibly small hawks, certainly cats, will come to hunt the birds. Spilled seeds, especially millet and the cereal grains in cheaper seed mixes, will sprout in your garden and flower beds, or the neighbors'.

None of this will be expensive, tedious, or a strain on neighborly good will if you manage things sensibly and keep priorities straight.

A reason sometimes given for not feeding is that you will lure summer birds into sticking around too long, and they will miss migration and die. The opposite is in fact true; well-fed song birds are more likely to migrate. A threshold level of body fat is believed to trigger migration departure in many species. Any migrants that stay around do so because they are sick, injured, or suffer some behavioral quirk that makes them stay. For such birds, having access to a feeder could save their lives.

Another truism about feeding is that once you start, you're honor-bound to keep it up, and that if you suddenly stop in mid-winter your trusting little friends will die.

If birds have become dependent on your feeder, they could die, but only in extremely cold weather and if yours is the only feeder in the vicinity. In such cases, your feeder could be crucial to small birds such as chickadees, who will add up to 10% of their body weight in fat during the day and burn it off at night to keep warm.

However, if you're one of several close neighbors who feed birds, the birds can relocate when one of you stops feeding. If you take a winter vacation, minimize relocation stress by letting feed run out during a mild weather spell in advance of your departure. Your trusting little friends will soon be back when you return.

Getting Started

Ask local birders what seeds they use and what species of birds they attract. Different parts of this vast continent have different winter birds which call for varying feeders and techniques. There are four basic feeder designs: hanging, post, table, and windowsill shelf. Some yards can hold all four; in others there is room for only one. It is wise to start small, resist the impulse to buy several, and wait for experience to tell you what is most appropriate for you.

What to Feed?

The closest-to-universal feed is black sunflower. At 40% oil content and with a good component of carbohydrates, it is great winter food and most birds love it. Do not use the confectionary or striped sunflower, which is hard for smaller birds to crack. Another quality feed, depending on the acquired preferences of your local birds, is white millet.

Mixing seed is perfectly fine as long as all the components are what your birds like. Supermarket mixes aren't usually adequate, containing cereal grains and other fillers along with regular seed. Quail and pheasants like this, but for them you're better off to buy "hen scratch" at the farm feed store. Cheap mixes attract the "RSPC" crowd—rats, starlings, pigeons, and crows. The birds you want to feed will flip through the junk to get the few sunflower seeds and/or millet, wasting the rest. If you want to offer a mix, buy the custom blends at the bird shop. Even these should only be offered on a table or large shelf where birds can select what they want without having to toss aside what they don't, as they will if you put mixes into tube or hanging feeders with small holes.

Suet is beef fat that can be put in a net bag or a wire cage feeder. It has special appeal to chickadees, nuthatches, jays, and woodpeckers. You can get it raw from the butcher and use it in rough chunks. You can also buy it rendered from the bird store in

If you don't want spilled bird seed to germinate in your yard, sterilize it in the oven for 30 minutes at 104° C (220° F).

a block which you can put into a net bag or in its own little metal cage. A cage is a good idea if you have crows, magpies, or jays. They'll rip a plastic bag to shreds and cart off all the suet in chunks.

Where to Feed?

Ideally, feeders should be placed where it's safest and most comfortable for the birds, and easy for you to watch from a convenient window. If you live in an area of really severe winters, try to get a spot that will offer shelter from the prevailing winds. On most lots, the house itself is the best windbreak. If you feed on a table or a shelf on a post, it can be self-sheltering with two high sides attached to adjacent edges of the platform, against the prevailing wind. A low raised rim around the other two edges will help keep the wind from whisking away the seeds. Carpet or coarse fabric holds seed better than a smooth wood surface, and so reduces blowaway.

In very wet climates, feeders should be placed under eaves, on a roofed table, or somehow fitted so water will not get onto the platform or into the feeding ports. Soaked seed won't feed through the holes in the feeding ports and quickly sprouts.

Speaking of Water ...

Fresh water offered in a shallow pan is a magnet for birds. Fitted with a pump, drip bucket, or mist sprayer that makes dripping or trickling noises, it is irresistible. The container should be shallow, or at least have some part of it covered by only a small amount of water, and the lining and rim should be rough to allow a good grip.

Keeping Your Feeder Hassle-Free

If you opt for the close, continuing relationship you get when you feed wild birds, you owe it to yourself, the birds, and your neighbors to be aware of potential problems and to take steps to prevent their occurrence.

The Ounce of Prevention

Poorly-stored seed causes much grief. A bag of it in the carport, porch, or woodshed will be sniffed out by rats or raccoons in no time. If you don't have a metal garden shed, your best buy is a steel garbage can with a solid lid. Plastic won't stop a rat's teeth for more than a few minutes. And once they find a food source, they stay and multiply. Be very careful to sweep up seed spilled where you don't want rats to move in.

Cats

It is a given that seeds will spill out of feeders onto the ground. Some birds will follow the seeds to wherever they land. If this is near where cats can hide, move the feeder to a spot where there is plenty of clear space around it, or move the hideaway. Otherwise, you are luring your birds into an ambush.

If the best place for the feeder has prized shrubbery near its base, you can cat-barrier this potential hideaway with woven wire. Put it up around the border of the shrubs, just high enough so that a cat hiding in the foliage behind will have to jump over it to get at the birds. This will give the birds a split-second warning, enough to make a getaway.

Another favorite cat trick is to lurk beneath a table or shelf feeder until birds land, when the cat will leap up over the edge and grab a bird before it can spring away.

You can foil this stunt in two ways. Place the feeder so that the platform is at least five feet (1.5 m) above the nearest launch point, or staple light woven wire to the feeder platform so that it extends horizontally for eight to ten inches (20 to 25 cm) all around the platform. When birds land on the wire they can see a cat pounce. If they're on the platform, the cat has to jump for the outer edge of the wire, then try to scramble over it. The wire might get bent, but the birds escape.

It is especially important to make a bath cat-unfriendly because birds using it are diverted and making a lot of noise, which both attracts attention and makes it impossible for them to hear and see a skulking predator.

Squirrels

Some people love them, others hate them. When you start feeding birds they will come calling. Depending on where you live your guests can include Red, Gray, Fox, or Flying Squirrels, or all four. Other members of the family include various ground squirrels, woodchucks, and those fleet little charmers, chipmunks.

Commercial "squirrel-proof" feeders come in great variety. Mounting them on poles that squirrels can't climb or adding a hubcap-shaped disk mounted like a wobbly collar on the pole are popular foils. On hanging feeders the suspending line is run through the center of a disk. Some have clever counterweighted gates that close off the feeder slot under the weight of a squirrel, but stay open for the lighter small birds.

However clever they are, feeders should be five feet (1.5 m) or more off the ground and eight feet (2.44 m) or more horizontal distance from the nearest tree or other elevated launch point, to keep squirrels from jumping up, across, or down to, the feeder.

For obvious reasons flying squirrels defy exclusion. They are not usually regarded as pests because they're active only after dark and don't hassle the birds. But they can chew through plastic or wood, and if they get into a feeder, they may sleep in the bin during the day. Feeders made of sturdy metal, or with metal rims on outlets, will keep these nocturnal nuisances from doing ruinous damage.

Diversionary feeding is an old trick. You offer the nuisance species a place of their own and stock it with feed that is cheaper than bird seed. Squirrels love corn, on or off the cob. Crows, pigeons, grackles, and starlings like "hen scratch" which you can dole out by the shovelful and make more tempting by serving it in a place that's easier for them to find.

If this seems too much like "aiding the enemy" you can enclose your feeders with a wire screen that lets the small species through, but bars pigeons and crows. Stucco wire with a two-inch mesh serves this purpose admirably.

Birdhouses and Shelters

Several species of birds have benefitted greatly from artificial houses. The most famous house birds are Purple Martins, followed closely by Bluebirds. Several species of wrens, notably the aptly named house wren, are enthusiastic house tenants, as is the widely distributed tree swallow.

For the aspiring bird landlord, bird stores stock plenty of models along with advice on how to use them. Some store-bought houses come in pre-cut kits, complete with nails and screws which, in the event you follow the instructions, assemble into a credibly trim box.

Plans abound if you're handy. You can go from the austere utilitarian models to truly imaginative creations. Don't, in the name of creativity, alter basic box dimensions and entrance hole size and placement. You should build to the needs of each species you hope to host; there is no one-size-fits-all birdhouse.

Because house plans are so easily obtainable none are given here. You can plan your own using the table of box dimensions and hole sizes on page 138. Beyond these basics, bear in mind that a house should keep the rain out, but have air holes for ventilation. Construction should be strong enough (use screws, not nails) to keep raccoons or small children from tearing them apart, but you should be able to easily remove either the roof or (preferably) the front panel to clear out mouse, sparrow, or starling nests and to houseclean between nesting seasons.

Using preservative-treated stock is probably not a good idea. Letting the wood weather to its natural state is a good idea. If you want to paint, just do the outside, and use a subdued neutral shade. Be sure to leave the inner surface of the entrance hole panel good and rough so that when the nestlings start flying, they have something to grip onto as they scramble out.

Agile raccoons, cats, and possums can stretch their paws well into a hole to snag nestlings. "Predator bars" are an extra thickness of material attached to the outside of the front wall. The entrance hole is bored through this extra layer, and so a tunnel is created to deter most nest robbers.

As well, squirrels like birdhouses as homes for themselves. Sandwiching a sheet of metal between the predator bar and the wall, with the hole in it an exact match of the one in the wood, will stop a squirrel from enlarging the hole.

Placement is another important safety feature. If the house is fixed to a tree, you may want to wrap two feet (60 cm) of the trunk right below the house with metal or plastic sheeting to keep climbers away. And, as with feeders, put them high enough (over five feet/ 1.5 m) off the ground to prevent cats from jumping up onto them and squatting on the roof.

Some birds may not be welcome tenants. The European Starling and the House Sparrow are noisy and messy. House Sparrows can harass bluebirds and martins out of house and home. Starlings will vanquish flickers and Red-Headed Woodpeckers from the holes they have laboriously excavated. These aggressive, prolific nuisances soon preempt every nest hole in the area, and will wipe out the population of the native cavity nesters.

A chickadee that is brooding its eggs in its nest cavity will try to scare off an intruder by hissing and waving its head back and forth like a snake.

To help native species, watch for sparrow and starling nests in buildings, and board up the entrance holes. If they move into your birdhouses, clean out their nest trash, or cover the holes, until they give up. Because the holes in Purple Martin houses are large enough for sparrows and starlings to get into, they should be plugged when the martins leave in the fall and opened again as soon as the van-guard returns in spring. Martins can defend their apartments once they've settled in, but if the claim jumpers get in first the martins may be unable to kick them out and will need some backup.

Summer's birdhouse can be converted into winter's roost shelter. Clean out the old nest stuff and install a perch—a small branch or thin doweling—up near the top of the cavity where there will still be enough head room. Plug the ventilator holes, and put the front panel back on with the entrance hole low down. Chickadees, nuthatches, Downy and Hairy Woodpeckers, sapsuckers, and other cavity nesters may find such a snug roost a haven from winter's harsh blasts.

Safety-Proofing Your Windows

Some of the deadliest traps we put up for birds are big windows and clear plastic panels around decks and porches.

Birds crash into windows for two reasons: the glass is a mirror, and birds try to fly into the trees and sky they see reflected in it; and windows allow birds to see right through the house or through a corner of it, and they try to fly through.

Either way, the bird will be either dazed or will lie quivering below the window. Despite its floppy-headed condition when you pick it up, its neck isn't broken. It's suffering from concussion.

If the bird is sitting upright, eyes open, and there are no nearby dangers, don't do anything for a moment or two. If it's livening up, it will shortly take off on its own. But if it appears to be down for the count, pick it up and put it in a secure place. In summer this can mean tucking it out of sight where a predator won't spot it. But if it's raining or very cold, put it in a small box with a few folds of toilet paper on the bottom and some holes for ventilation, close the lid, and bring the bird inside. Put it where it won't be disturbed.

When you hear it stirring about, don't open the box indoors; the bird will escape and knock itself out again trying to fly through the nearest window. Take the closed box outside. If the bird has recovered it will spring out and fly away. If it's still alive, but groggy, close the lid again and give it more quiet time.

Cats, crows, etc. quickly learn that the whacking sound could mean an easy catch. Some hawks, crows, and other winged opportunists will buzz feeders near the house to panic the birds into bashing into a window.

The real solution is to prevent collisions from occurring in the first place. Some windows, even large ones, seem never to generate hits. Others, even small ones, are real killers.

Birding lore abounds with deterrents such as putting a hawk silhouette, or a couple of round colored discs, or strips of plastic tape on the outside surface of the glass. These may work, but often they have no effect whatever.

The Northern Flicker, a woodpecker that drills holes in trees for nesting, nevertheless forages mostly on the ground, in search of ants.

The no-fail cure is to put up a barrier that birds can't miss. The least intrusive is plastic garden netting. You can staple it to a frame the same size as the window frame, and install it during the bird season as you would storm windows or screens.

If you feed birds, you may have the window-hit problem all year round, especially if you have a large table feeder positioned so that birds flaring from it in panic might collide with the window. You can lessen this hazard by moving the feeder. Or, you can do the opposite by putting a shelf feeder right on the windowsill. Birds using it will quickly and without fatal results learn that the glass is there. Even if they flare off the shelf into the glass they won't have enough momentum to harm themselves.

Wild animals living and feeding near roads become accustomed to vehicles. Your car is therefore a very good "blind" from which to observe them.

NOTES ON
NEW BIRD SIGHTINGS
with quick-sketch outlines

Note: Our *Birder's Journal* brings you a new idea to help make field identification of new birds quicker and more accurate. These are our "quick-sketch outlines," which are partially-completed, basic illustrations of four generic bird forms. Many birders, upon seeing a new bird, don't waste time flipping through the pages of a field guide. Instead, they make a quick sketch, trying to note key marks while the bird is still in view. Then they check the field guide, relying on their sketch for critical cues.

Our "quick-sketch outlines" (on the left-hand page) do part of the job for you, and the reminder checklist (on the right-hand page) provides a list of basic body characteristics, so you can spend your time marking critical details instead of the basic body outline. Have fun!

Shorebird

Relative size

Waterfowl

Relative size

28

Sighting

Species	Number
Date	Time
Weather	Place

Habitat

Description

Call/Song

Behavior

Field Guide Page Number

Checklist for Sketches

Head: Crest? Color? Bill? (*length, color, shape*) Eye? (*dark, color, stripe*)

Neck: Length? Color?	**Breast**: Color(s)? Pattern?
Back: Color(s)? Pattern?	**Wing**: Color(s)? Length? Bars?
Belly: Color(s)? Pattern?	**Rump**: Color(s)?
Tail: Color(s)?	**Under-tail Coverts**: Color(s)?

Legs: Color? Length?

Bird of prey

Relative size

Songbird

Relative size

Sighting

Species _____ Number _____

Date _____ Time _____

Weather _____ Place _____

Habitat _____

Description _____

_____

_____

_____

_____

Call/Song _____

_____

Behavior _____

_____

_____

Field Guide Page Number _____

Checklist for Sketches

Head: Crest? Color? Bill? *(length, color, shape)* Eye? *(dark, color, stripe)*

Neck: Length? Color?	**Breast**: Color(s)? Pattern?
Back: Color(s)? Pattern?	**Wing**: Color(s)? Length? Bars?
Belly: Color(s)? Pattern?	**Rump**: Color(s)?
Tail: Color(s)?	**Under-tail Coverts**: Color(s)?
Legs: Color? Length?	

Shorebird

Relative size

Waterfowl

Relative size

Sighting

Species _____ Number _____

Date _____ Time _____

Weather _____ Place _____

Habitat _____

Description _____

_____

_____

_____

Call/Song _____

Behavior _____

_____

Field Guide Page Number _____

Checklist for Sketches

Head: Crest? Color? Bill? *(length, color, shape)* Eye? *(dark, color, stripe)*

Neck: Length? Color?	**Breast**: Color(s)? Pattern?
Back: Color(s)? Pattern?	**Wing**: Color(s)? Length? Bars?
Belly: Color(s)? Pattern?	**Rump**: Color(s)?
Tail: Color(s)?	**Under-tail Coverts**: Color(s)?

Legs: Color? Length?

Bird of prey

Relative size

Songbird

Relative size

Sighting

Species _____ Number _____

Date _____ Time _____

Weather _____ Place _____

Habitat _____

Description _____

_____

_____

_____

_____

Call/Song _____

_____

Behavior _____

_____

_____

Field Guide Page Number _____

Checklist for Sketches

Head: Crest? Color? Bill? *(length, color, shape)* Eye? *(dark, color, stripe)*

Neck: Length? Color?	**Breast**: Color(s)? Pattern?
Back: Color(s)? Pattern?	**Wing**: Color(s)? Length? Bars?
Belly: Color(s)? Pattern?	**Rump**: Color(s)?
Tail: Color(s)?	**Under-tail Coverts**: Color(s)?
Legs: Color? Length?	

Shorebird

Relative size

Waterfowl

Relative size

Sighting

Species _____ Number _____

Date _____ Time _____

Weather _____ Place _____

Habitat _____

Description _____

_____

_____

_____

Call/Song _____

_____

Behavior _____

_____

Field Guide Page Number _____

Checklist for Sketches

Head: Crest? Color? Bill? (*length, color, shape*) Eye? (*dark, color, stripe*)

Neck: Length? Color?	**Breast**: Color(s)? Pattern?
Back: Color(s)? Pattern?	**Wing**: Color(s)? Length? Bars?
Belly: Color(s)? Pattern?	**Rump**: Color(s)?
Tail: Color(s)?	**Under-tail Coverts**: Color(s)?
Legs: Color? Length?	

Bird of prey

Relative size

Songbird

Relative size

Sighting

Species	Number
Date	Time
Weather	Place

Habitat

Description

Call/Song

Behavior

Field Guide Page Number

Checklist for Sketches

Head: Crest? Color? Bill? (*length, color, shape*) Eye? (*dark, color, stripe*)

Neck: Length? Color?	**Breast**: Color(s)? Pattern?
Back: Color(s)? Pattern?	**Wing**: Color(s)? Length? Bars?
Belly: Color(s)? Pattern?	**Rump**: Color(s)?
Tail: Color(s)?	**Under-tail Coverts**: Color(s)?

Legs: Color? Length?

Shorebird

Relative size

Waterfowl

Relative size

40

Sighting

Species	Number
Date	Time
Weather	Place
Habitat	

Description

Call/Song

Behavior

Field Guide Page Number

Checklist for Sketches

Head: Crest? Color? Bill? (*length, color, shape*) Eye? (*dark, color, stripe*)

Neck: Length? Color?	**Breast**: Color(s)? Pattern?
Back: Color(s)? Pattern?	**Wing**: Color(s)? Length? Bars?
Belly: Color(s)? Pattern?	**Rump**: Color(s)?
Tail: Color(s)?	**Under-tail Coverts**: Color(s)?
Legs: Color? Length?	

Bird of prey

Relative size

Songbird

Relative size

Sighting

Species	Number
Date	Time
Weather	Place

Habitat

Description

Call/Song

Behavior

Field Guide Page Number

Checklist for Sketches

Head: Crest? Color? Bill? (*length, color, shape*) Eye? (*dark, color, stripe*)

Neck: Length? Color?	**Breast**: Color(s)? Pattern?
Back: Color(s)? Pattern?	**Wing**: Color(s)? Length? Bars?
Belly: Color(s)? Pattern?	**Rump**: Color(s)?
Tail: Color(s)?	**Under-tail Coverts**: Color(s)?

Legs: Color? Length?

Shorebird

Relative size

Waterfowl

Relative size

Sighting

Species	Number
Date	Time
Weather	Place

Habitat

Description

Call/Song

Behavior

Field Guide Page Number

Checklist for Sketches

Head: Crest? Color? Bill? (*length, color, shape*) Eye? (*dark, color, stripe*)

Neck: Length? Color?	**Breast**: Color(s)? Pattern?
Back: Color(s)? Pattern?	**Wing**: Color(s)? Length? Bars?
Belly: Color(s)? Pattern?	**Rump**: Color(s)?
Tail: Color(s)?	**Under-tail Coverts**: Color(s)?

Legs: Color? Length?

Bird of prey

Relative size

Songbird

Relative size

46

Sighting

Species	Number
Date	Time
Weather	Place
Habitat	

Description

Call/Song

Behavior

Field Guide Page Number

Checklist for Sketches

Head: Crest? Color? Bill? (*length, color, shape*) Eye? (*dark, color, stripe*)

Neck: Length? Color?	**Breast**: Color(s)? Pattern?
Back: Color(s)? Pattern?	**Wing**: Color(s)? Length? Bars?
Belly: Color(s)? Pattern?	**Rump**: Color(s)?
Tail: Color(s)?	**Under-tail Coverts**: Color(s)?
Legs: Color? Length?	

Shorebird   *Relative size*

Waterfowl   *Relative size*

Sighting

Species	Number
Date	Time
Weather	Place

Habitat

Description

Call/Song

Behavior

Field Guide Page Number

Checklist for Sketches

Head: Crest? Color? Bill? (*length, color, shape*) Eye? (*dark, color, stripe*)

Neck: Length? Color?	**Breast**: Color(s)? Pattern?
Back: Color(s)? Pattern?	**Wing**: Color(s)? Length? Bars?
Belly: Color(s)? Pattern?	**Rump**: Color(s)?
Tail: Color(s)?	**Under-tail Coverts**: Color(s)?

Legs: Color? Length?

Bird of prey

Relative size

Songbird

Relative size

Sighting

Species _____ Number _____

Date _____ Time _____

Weather _____ Place _____

Habitat _____

Description _____

_____

_____

_____

Call/Song _____

_____

Behavior _____

_____

Field Guide Page Number _____

Checklist for Sketches

Head: Crest? Color? Bill? *(length, color, shape)* Eye? *(dark, color, stripe)*

Neck: Length? Color?	**Breast**: Color(s)? Pattern?
Back: Color(s)? Pattern?	**Wing**: Color(s)? Length? Bars?
Belly: Color(s)? Pattern?	**Rump**: Color(s)?
Tail: Color(s)?	**Under-tail Coverts**: Color(s)?

Legs: Color? Length?

Shorebird

Relative size

Waterfowl

Relative size

Sighting

Species _____ Number _____

Date _____ Time _____

Weather _____ Place _____

Habitat _____

Description _____

_____

_____

_____

Call/Song _____

Behavior _____

_____

Field Guide Page Number _____

Checklist for Sketches

Head: Crest? Color? Bill? *(length, color, shape)* Eye? *(dark, color, stripe)*

Neck: Length? Color?	**Breast**: Color(s)? Pattern?
Back: Color(s)? Pattern?	**Wing**: Color(s)? Length? Bars?
Belly: Color(s)? Pattern?	**Rump**: Color(s)?
Tail: Color(s)?	**Under-tail Coverts**: Color(s)?

Legs: Color? Length?

Bird of prey

Relative size

Songbird

Relative size

54

Sighting

Species _____ Number _____

Date _____ Time _____

Weather _____ Place _____

Habitat _____

Description _____

_____

_____

_____

Call/Song _____

Behavior _____

_____

Field Guide Page Number _____

Checklist for Sketches

Head: Crest? Color? Bill? (*length, color, shape*) Eye? (*dark, color, stripe*)

Neck: Length? Color?	**Breast**: Color(s)? Pattern?
Back: Color(s)? Pattern?	**Wing**: Color(s)? Length? Bars?
Belly: Color(s)? Pattern?	**Rump**: Color(s)?
Tail: Color(s)?	**Under-tail Coverts**: Color(s)?

Legs: Color? Length?

Shorebird

Relative size

Waterfowl

Relative size

Sighting

Species _____ Number _____

Date _____ Time _____

Weather _____ Place _____

Habitat _____

Description _____

_____

_____

_____

Call/Song _____

Behavior _____

_____

Field Guide Page Number _____

Checklist for Sketches

Head: Crest? Color? Bill? (_length, color, shape_) Eye? (_dark, color, stripe_)

Neck: Length? Color?   **Breast**: Color(s)? Pattern?

Back: Color(s)? Pattern?   **Wing**: Color(s)? Length? Bars?

Belly: Color(s)? Pattern?   **Rump**: Color(s)?

Tail: Color(s)?   **Under-tail Coverts**: Color(s)?

Legs: Color? Length?

Bird of prey

Relative size

Songbird

Relative size

58

Sighting

Species _____ Number _____

Date _____ Time _____

Weather _____ Place _____

Habitat _____

Description _____

Call/Song _____

Behavior _____

Field Guide Page Number _____

Checklist for Sketches

Head: Crest? Color? Bill? (*length, color, shape*) Eye? (*dark, color, stripe*)

Neck: Length? Color?   **Breast**: Color(s)? Pattern?

Back: Color(s)? Pattern?   **Wing**: Color(s)? Length? Bars?

Belly: Color(s)? Pattern?   **Rump**: Color(s)?

Tail: Color(s)?   **Under-tail Coverts**: Color(s)?

Legs: Color? Length?

Shorebird

Relative size

Waterfowl

Relative size

60

Sighting

Species	Number
Date	Time
Weather	Place
Habitat	

Description

Call/Song

Behavior

Field Guide Page Number

Checklist for Sketches

Head: Crest? Color? Bill? *(length, color, shape)* Eye? *(dark, color, stripe)*

Neck: Length? Color?	**Breast**: Color(s)? Pattern?
Back: Color(s)? Pattern?	**Wing**: Color(s)? Length? Bars?
Belly: Color(s)? Pattern?	**Rump**: Color(s)?
Tail: Color(s)?	**Under-tail Coverts**: Color(s)?
Legs: Color? Length?	

Bird of prey

Relative size

Songbird

Relative size

62

Sighting

Species _____ Number _____

Date _____ Time _____

Weather _____ Place _____

Habitat _____

Description _____

Call/Song _____

Behavior _____

Field Guide Page Number _____

Checklist for Sketches

Head: Crest? Color? Bill? (_length, color, shape_) Eye? (_dark, color, stripe_)

Neck: Length? Color?	**Breast**: Color(s)? Pattern?
Back: Color(s)? Pattern?	**Wing**: Color(s)? Length? Bars?
Belly: Color(s)? Pattern?	**Rump**: Color(s)?
Tail: Color(s)?	**Under-tail Coverts**: Color(s)?

Legs: Color? Length?

Shorebird   Relative size

Waterfowl   Relative size

64

Sighting

Species	Number
Date	Time
Weather	Place
Habitat	

Description

Call/Song

Behavior

Field Guide Page Number

Checklist for Sketches

Head: Crest? Color? Bill? (*length, color, shape*) Eye? (*dark, color, stripe*)

Neck: Length? Color?	**Breast**: Color(s)? Pattern?
Back: Color(s)? Pattern?	**Wing**: Color(s)? Length? Bars?
Belly: Color(s)? Pattern?	**Rump**: Color(s)?
Tail: Color(s)?	**Under-tail Coverts**: Color(s)?

Legs: Color? Length?

Bird of prey

Relative size

Songbird

Relative size

Sighting

Species _____ Number _____

Date _____ Time _____

Weather _____ Place _____

Habitat _____

Description _____

_____

_____

_____

Call/Song _____

Behavior _____

_____

Field Guide Page Number _____

Checklist for Sketches

Head: Crest? Color? Bill? (*length, color, shape*) Eye? (*dark, color, stripe*)

Neck: Length? Color? | **Breast**: Color(s)? Pattern?

Back: Color(s)? Pattern? | **Wing**: Color(s)? Length? Bars?

Belly: Color(s)? Pattern? | **Rump**: Color(s)?

Tail: Color(s)? | **Under-tail Coverts**: Color(s)?

Legs: Color? Length?

Shorebird

Relative size

Waterfowl

Relative size

68

Sighting

Species _____ Number _____

Date _____ Time _____

Weather _____ Place _____

Habitat _____

Description _____

Call/Song _____

Behavior _____

Field Guide Page Number _____

Checklist for Sketches

Head: Crest? Color? Bill? *(length, color, shape)* Eye? *(dark, color, stripe)*

Neck: Length? Color?   **Breast**: Color(s)? Pattern?

Back: Color(s)? Pattern?   **Wing**: Color(s)? Length? Bars?

Belly: Color(s)? Pattern?   **Rump**: Color(s)?

Tail: Color(s)?   **Under-tail Coverts**: Color(s)?

Legs: Color? Length?

Bird of prey

Relative size

Songbird

Relative size

70

Sighting

Species	Number
Date	Time
Weather	Place
Habitat	

Description

Call/Song

Behavior

Field Guide Page Number

Checklist for Sketches

Head: Crest? Color? Bill? (*length, color, shape*) Eye? (*dark, color, stripe*)

Neck: Length? Color?	**Breast**: Color(s)? Pattern?
Back: Color(s)? Pattern?	**Wing**: Color(s)? Length? Bars?
Belly: Color(s)? Pattern?	**Rump**: Color(s)?
Tail: Color(s)?	**Under-tail Coverts**: Color(s)?

Legs: Color? Length?

Shorebird

Relative size

Waterfowl

Relative size

Sighting

Species _____ Number _____

Date _____ Time _____

Weather _____ Place _____

Habitat _____

Description _____

_____

_____

_____

Call/Song _____

Behavior _____

_____

Field Guide Page Number _____

Checklist for Sketches

Head: Crest? Color? Bill? *(length, color, shape)* Eye? *(dark, color, stripe)*

Neck: Length? Color?   **Breast**: Color(s)? Pattern?

Back: Color(s)? Pattern?   **Wing**: Color(s)? Length? Bars?

Belly: Color(s)? Pattern?   **Rump**: Color(s)?

Tail: Color(s)?   **Under-tail Coverts**: Color(s)?

Legs: Color? Length?

Bird of prey

Relative size

Songbird

Relative size

74

Sighting

Species _____ Number _____

Date _____ Time _____

Weather _____ Place _____

Habitat _____

_____

Description _____

_____

_____

_____

_____

Call/Song _____

_____

Behavior _____

_____

_____

Field Guide Page Number _____

_____

Checklist for Sketches

Head: Crest? Color? Bill? (_length, color, shape_) Eye? (_dark, color, stripe_)

Neck: Length? Color? | **Breast**: Color(s)? Pattern?

Back: Color(s)? Pattern? | **Wing**: Color(s)? Length? Bars?

Belly: Color(s)? Pattern? | **Rump**: Color(s)?

Tail: Color(s)? | **Under-tail Coverts**: Color(s)?

Legs: Color? Length?

Shorebird   *Relative size*

Waterfowl   *Relative size*

Sighting

Species	Number
Date	Time
Weather	Place

Habitat

Description

Call/Song

Behavior

Field Guide Page Number

Checklist for Sketches

Head: Crest? Color? Bill? *(length, color, shape)* Eye? *(dark, color, stripe)*

Neck: Length? Color?	**Breast**: Color(s)? Pattern?
Back: Color(s)? Pattern?	**Wing**: Color(s)? Length? Bars?
Belly: Color(s)? Pattern?	**Rump**: Color(s)?
Tail: Color(s)?	**Under-tail Coverts**: Color(s)?
Legs: Color? Length?	

Bird of prey

Relative size

Songbird

Relative size

Sighting

Species _____ Number _____

Date _____ Time _____

Weather _____ Place _____

Habitat _____

Description _____

_____

_____

_____

Call/Song _____

Behavior _____

_____

Field Guide Page Number _____

Checklist for Sketches

Head: Crest? Color? Bill? *(length, color, shape)* Eye? *(dark, color, stripe)*

Neck: Length? Color?	**Breast**: Color(s)? Pattern?
Back: Color(s)? Pattern?	**Wing**: Color(s)? Length? Bars?
Belly: Color(s)? Pattern?	**Rump**: Color(s)?
Tail: Color(s)?	**Under-tail Coverts**: Color(s)?
Legs: Color? Length?	

Shorebird

Relative size

Waterfowl

Relative size

Sighting

Species _____ Number _____

Date _____ Time _____

Weather _____ Place _____

Habitat _____

Description _____

_____

_____

_____

Call/Song _____

_____

Behavior _____

_____

_____

Field Guide Page Number _____

Checklist for Sketches

Head: Crest? Color? Bill? *(length, color, shape)* Eye? *(dark, color, stripe)*

Neck: Length? Color? | **Breast**: Color(s)? Pattern?

Back: Color(s)? Pattern? | **Wing**: Color(s)? Length? Bars?

Belly: Color(s)? Pattern? | **Rump**: Color(s)?

Tail: Color(s)? | **Under-tail Coverts**: Color(s)?

Legs: Color? Length?

Bird of prey

Relative size

Songbird

Relative size

82

Sighting

Species	Number
Date	Time
Weather	Place
Habitat	

Description

Call/Song

Behavior

Field Guide Page Number

Checklist for Sketches

Head: Crest? Color? Bill? *(length, color, shape)* Eye? *(dark, color, stripe)*

Neck: Length? Color?	**Breast**: Color(s)? Pattern?
Back: Color(s)? Pattern?	**Wing**: Color(s)? Length? Bars?
Belly: Color(s)? Pattern?	**Rump**: Color(s)?
Tail: Color(s)?	**Under-tail Coverts**: Color(s)?

Legs: Color? Length?

Shorebird

Relative size

Waterfowl

Relative size

Sighting

Species _____ Number _____

Date _____ Time _____

Weather _____ Place _____

Habitat _____

Description _____

_____

_____

_____

Call/Song _____

Behavior _____

_____

Field Guide Page Number _____

Checklist for Sketches

Head: Crest? Color? Bill? *(length, color, shape)* Eye? *(dark, color, stripe)*

Neck: Length? Color?	**Breast**: Color(s)? Pattern?
Back: Color(s)? Pattern?	**Wing**: Color(s)? Length? Bars?
Belly: Color(s)? Pattern?	**Rump**: Color(s)?
Tail: Color(s)?	**Under-tail Coverts**: Color(s)?
Legs: Color? Length?	

Bird of prey

Relative size

Songbird

Relative size

Sighting

Species _____ Number _____

Date _____ Time _____

Weather _____ Place _____

Habitat _____

Description _____

_____

_____

_____

_____

Call/Song _____

_____

Behavior _____

_____

_____

Field Guide Page Number _____

Checklist for Sketches

Head: Crest? Color? Bill? (*length, color, shape*) Eye? (*dark, color, stripe*)

Neck: Length? Color?   **Breast**: Color(s)? Pattern?

Back: Color(s)? Pattern?   **Wing**: Color(s)? Length? Bars?

Belly: Color(s)? Pattern?   **Rump**: Color(s)?

Tail: Color(s)?   **Under-tail Coverts**: Color(s)?

Legs: Color? Length?

Shorebird

Relative size

Waterfowl

Relative size

88

Sighting

Species	Number
Date	Time
Weather	Place
Habitat	

Description

Call/Song

Behavior

Field Guide Page Number

Checklist for Sketches

Head: Crest? Color? Bill? *(length, color, shape)* Eye? *(dark, color, stripe)*

Neck: Length? Color?   **Breast**: Color(s)? Pattern?

Back: Color(s)? Pattern?   **Wing**: Color(s)? Length? Bars?

Belly: Color(s)? Pattern?   **Rump**: Color(s)?

Tail: Color(s)?   **Under-tail Coverts**: Color(s)?

Legs: Color? Length?

Bird of prey

Relative size

Songbird

Relative size

90

Sighting

Species _____ Number _____

Date _____ Time _____

Weather _____ Place _____

Habitat _____

Description _____

Call/Song _____

Behavior _____

Field Guide Page Number _____

Checklist for Sketches

Head: Crest? Color? Bill? *(length, color, shape)* Eye? *(dark, color, stripe)*

Neck: Length? Color?   **Breast**: Color(s)? Pattern?

Back: Color(s)? Pattern?   **Wing**: Color(s)? Length? Bars?

Belly: Color(s)? Pattern?   **Rump**: Color(s)?

Tail: Color(s)?   **Under-tail Coverts**: Color(s)?

Legs: Color? Length?

Shorebird

Relative size

Waterfowl

Relative size

Sighting

Species _____ Number _____

Date _____ Time _____

Weather _____ Place _____

Habitat _____

Description _____

_____

_____

_____

Call/Song _____

Behavior _____

_____

Field Guide Page Number _____

Checklist for Sketches

Head: Crest? Color? Bill? (*length, color, shape*) Eye? (*dark, color, stripe*)

Neck: Length? Color?	**Breast**: Color(s)? Pattern?
Back: Color(s)? Pattern?	**Wing**: Color(s)? Length? Bars?
Belly: Color(s)? Pattern?	**Rump**: Color(s)?
Tail: Color(s)?	**Under-tail Coverts**: Color(s)?
Legs: Color? Length?	

Bird of prey

Relative size

Songbird

Relative size

Sighting

Species _____ Number _____

Date _____ Time _____

Weather _____ Place _____

Habitat _____

Description _____

_____

_____

_____

Call/Song _____

_____

Behavior _____

_____

Field Guide Page Number _____

Checklist for Sketches

Head: Crest? Color? Bill? *(length, color, shape)* Eye? *(dark, color, stripe)*

Neck: Length? Color? **Breast**: Color(s)? Pattern?

Back: Color(s)? Pattern? **Wing**: Color(s)? Length? Bars?

Belly: Color(s)? Pattern? **Rump**: Color(s)?

Tail: Color(s)? **Under-tail Coverts**: Color(s)?

Legs: Color? Length?

Sighting

Species _____ Number _____

Date _____ Time _____

Weather _____ Place _____

Habitat _____

Description _____

Call/Song _____

Behavior _____

Field Guide Page Number _____

Checklist for sketches

Head: Crest? Colour? Bill? (*length, color, shape*) Eye? (*dark, color, stripe*)

Neck: Length? Color?	**Breast**: Color(s)? Pattern?
Back: Color(s)? Pattern?	**Wing**: Color(s)? Length? Bars?
Belly: Color(s)? Pattern?	**Rump**: Color(s)?
Tail: Color(s)?	**Under-tail Coverts**: Color(s)?

Legs: Color? Length?

Sighting

Species _____ Number _____

Date _____ Time _____

Weather _____ Place _____

Habitat _____

Description _____

Call/Song _____

Behavior _____

Field Guide Page Number _____

Checklist for sketches

Head: Crest? Colour? Bill? (*length, color, shape*) Eye? (*dark, color, stripe*)

Neck: Length? Color?	**Breast**: Color(s)? Pattern?
Back: Color(s)? Pattern?	**Wing**: Color(s)? Length? Bars?
Belly: Color(s)? Pattern?	**Rump**: Color(s)?
Tail: Color(s)?	**Under-tail Coverts**: Color(s)?
Legs: Color? Length?	

Sighting

Species _____ Number _____

Date _____ Time _____

Weather _____ Place _____

Habitat _____

Description _____

_____

_____

_____

Call/Song _____

Behavior _____

_____

Field Guide Page Number _____

Checklist for sketches

Head: Crest? Colour? Bill? (*length, color, shape*) Eye? (*dark, color, stripe*)

Neck: Length? Color?	**Breast**: Color(s)? Pattern?
Back: Color(s)? Pattern?	**Wing**: Color(s)? Length? Bars?
Belly: Color(s)? Pattern?	**Rump**: Color(s)?
Tail: Color(s)?	**Under-tail Coverts**: Color(s)?
Legs: Color? Length?	

Sighting

Species	Number
Date	Time
Weather	Place
Habitat	

Description

Call/Song

Behavior

Field Guide Page Number

Checklist for sketches

Head: Crest? Colour? Bill? (*length, color, shape*) Eye? (*dark, color, stripe*)

Neck: Length? Color?	**Breast**: Color(s)? Pattern?
Back: Color(s)? Pattern?	**Wing**: Color(s)? Length? Bars?
Belly: Color(s)? Pattern?	**Rump**: Color(s)?
Tail: Color(s)?	**Under-tail Coverts**: Color(s)?
Legs: Color? Length?	

Sighting

Species	Number
Date	Time
Weather	Place

Habitat

Description

Call/Song

Behavior

Field Guide Page Number

Checklist for sketches

Head: Crest? Colour? Bill? (*length, color, shape*) Eye? (*dark, color, stripe*)

Neck: Length? Color?	**Breast**: Color(s)? Pattern?
Back: Color(s)? Pattern?	**Wing**: Color(s)? Length? Bars?
Belly: Color(s)? Pattern?	**Rump**: Color(s)?
Tail: Color(s)?	**Under-tail Coverts**: Color(s)?
Legs: Color? Length?	

Sighting

Species _____ Number _____

Date _____ Time _____

Weather _____ Place _____

Habitat _____

_____

Description _____

_____

_____

_____

_____

Call/Song _____

_____

Behavior _____

_____

_____

Field Guide Page Number _____

_____

Checklist for sketches

Head: Crest? Colour? Bill? *(length, color, shape)* Eye? *(dark, color, stripe)*

Neck: Length? Color?   **Breast**: Color(s)? Pattern?

Back: Color(s)? Pattern?   **Wing**: Color(s)? Length? Bars?

Belly: Color(s)? Pattern?   **Rump**: Color(s)?

Tail: Color(s)?   **Under-tail Coverts**: Color(s)?

Legs: Color? Length?

NOTES ON BIRDING TRIPS

Date(s) _____ Weather _____

Place _____

How to Get There _____

_____

_____

Friends _____

Species	Number

Notes _____

_____

_____

Date(s) _____ Weather _____

Place _____

How to Get There _____

_____

_____

Friends _____

Species	Number

Notes _____

_____

_____

Date(s)_____ Weather _____

Place _____

How to Get There _____

_____

_____

Friends _____

Species	Number

Notes _____

_____

_____

112

Date(s) _____ Weather _____

Place _____

How to Get There _____

_____

_____

Friends _____

Species	Number

Notes _____

_____

_____

Date(s) _____ Weather _____

Place _____

How to Get There _____

_____

_____

Friends _____

Species	Number

Notes _____

_____

_____

Date(s) _____ Weather _____

Place _____

How to Get There _____

_____

_____

Friends _____

Species	Number

Notes _____

_____

_____

Date(s) _____ Weather _____

Place _____

How to Get There _____

_____

_____

Friends _____

Species	Number

Notes _____

_____

_____

Date(s) _____ Weather _____

Place _____

How to Get There _____

_____

_____

Friends _____

Species	Number

Notes _____

_____

_____

Date(s) _____ Weather _____

Place _____

How to Get There _____

_____

_____

Friends _____

Species	Number

Notes _____

_____

_____

Date(s) _____ Weather _____

Place _____

How to Get There _____

_____

_____

Friends _____

Species	Number

Notes _____

_____

_____

Date(s) _____ Weather _____

Place _____

How to Get There _____

_____

_____

Friends _____

Species	Number

Notes _____

_____

_____

Date(s) _____ Weather _____

Place _____

How to Get There _____

_____

_____

Friends _____

Species	Number

Notes _____

_____

_____

NOTES ON
BIRDS AT THE FEEDER

Date(s) _____

Weather _____

_____

Seed Used _____

Species	Number

Notes _____

_____

_____

Date(s) _____

Weather _____

_____

Seed Used _____

Species	Number

Notes _____

_____

_____

Date(s)

Weather

Seed Used

Species	Number

Notes

Date(s)

Weather

Seed Used

Species	Number

Notes

Date(s)

Weather

Seed Used

Species	Number

Notes

Date(s) _____

Weather _____

_____

Seed Used _____

Species	Number

Notes _____

_____

_____

Date(s)

Weather

Seed Used

Species	Number

Notes

Date(s)

Weather

Seed Used

Species	Number

Notes

Date(s)

Weather

Seed Used

Species	Number

Notes

Date(s) _____

Weather _____

Seed Used _____

Species	Number

Notes _____

_____

_____

Date(s)

Weather

Seed Used

Species	Number

Notes

Date(s) _____

Weather _____

_____

Seed Used _____

Species	Number

Notes _____

_____

_____

Date(s) _____

Weather _____
_____

Seed Used _____

Species	Number

Notes _____
_____
_____

136

Date(s)

Weather

Seed Used

Species	Number

Notes

Birdhouse Dimensions
for Common Species

In cutting stock, allow for overlaps, sloped roofs, and longer
backpieces for attaching the finished house to a post or tree.
Stock should be ¾" (1.9 cm) thick or more to provide adequate
insulation from cold and heat. Outdoor plywood resists warping.
Drill the entrance hole so that the top of it is about an inch
(2.5 cm) below the roof. Make four ¼" (.6 cm) holes in the floor
for drainage and ventilation.

Inside Box Dimensions

Species	Entrance	Floor Size	Depth
Bluebird			
(Eastern)	1½" / 3.8 cm	5" x 5" / 12.7 cm	12" / 30.5 cm
(Mountain)	1⁹⁄₁₆" / 3.95 cm	5" x 5" / 12.7 cm	12" / 30.5 cm
(Western)	1⁹⁄₁₆" / 3.95 cm	5" x 5" / 12.7 cm	12" / 30.5 cm
Chickadee/	1¼" / 3.18 cm	4" x 4" / 10 cm	10" / 25.4 cm
titmouse			
House Finch	1½" / 3.8 cm	5" x 5" / 12.7 cm	10" / 25.4 cm
Nuthatches	1½" / 3.8 cm	4" x 4" / 10 cm	10" / 25.4 cm
Tree Swallow	1½" / 3.8 cm	5" x 5" / 12.7 cm	10" / 25.4 cm
Wren			
(House)	1" / 2.5 cm	4" x 4" / 10 cm	8" / 20.3 cm
(Carolina)	1¼" / 3.18 cm	4" x 4" / 10 cm	8" / 20.3 cm

*NB: Purple Martin house dimensions are not offered here because these are built like hotels with many
individual compartments under one roof. For plans, contact the Purple Martin Conservation
Association (refer to page 140).*

References

Birding/Naturalist Organizations

American Birding Association
PO Box 6599
Colorado Springs, CO
U.S.A. 80934
Phone (800) 850-2473 or (719) 578-1614 Fax (719) 578-1480
E-mail (sales): abasales@abasales.com

Canadian Nature Federation
520–1 Nicholas St
Ottawa, ON
Canada K1N 7B7
Phone (613) 562-3447   Fax (613) 562-3371
E-mail: cnf@web.net Web site: http://www.web.net/~cnf

Cornell Lab of Ornithology
159 Sapsucker Woods Road
Ithaca, NY
U.S.A. 14850
Phone (607) 254-BIRD

National Audubon Society
700 Broadway
New York, NY
U.S.A. 10003-9562
Phone (212) 979-3000 Fax (212) 979-3188

North American Bluebird Society
PO Box 74
Darlington, WI
U.S.A. 53530-0074
Phone (608) 329-6403 Fax (608) 329-7057
E-mail: nabluebird@aol.com
Web site: http://www.cobleskill.edu/nabs/

Purple Martin Conservation Association
Edinboro University of Pennsylvania
Edinboro, PA
U.S.A. 16444
Phone: (814) 734-4420
Web-site: http://www.purplemartin.org

Festivals

Directory of Birding Festivals
National Fish and Wildlife Foundation
1120 Connecticut Ave. NW, Suite 900
Washington, DC
U.S.A. 20036
Phone (202) 857-0166   Fax 857-0162
E-mail: info@nfwf.org   Web site: http://www.nfwf.org

Equipment List

Notes